Mary Dicin

with love from

Sam

THE SECRET OF TIPPITY-WITCHIT

JAMES ROOSE-EVANS
THE SECRET OF TIPPITY WITCHIT
AN ODD & ELSEWHERE STORY
WITH PICTURES BY BRIAN ROBB
ANDRE DEUTSCH

First published 1975 by
André Deutsch Limited
105 Great Russell Street London WC1

Printed in Great Britain by
Cox & Wyman Ltd
London Fakenham and Reading

ISBN 0 233 96683 8

THIS, THE SIXTH ODD AND ELSEWHERE BOOK
IS FOR
BARBARA WILKES
WHO FIRST MADE ODD AND ELSEWHERE AND
SO SET THE BOOKS IN MOTION

The first five books of Odd and Elsewhere are

THE ADVENTURES OF ODD AND ELSEWHERE

THE SECRET OF THE SEVEN BRIGHT SHINERS

ODD AND THE GREAT BEAR

ELSEWHERE AND THE GATHERING OF THE CLOWNS

THE RETURN OF THE GREAT BEAR

It was a misty autumn day. The trees had emptied all their leaves on to the lawn at Fenton House in Hampstead, and Hallelujah Jones, the gardener, was busy raking them up. The blue smoke from his bonfire drifted slowly across the garden.

In the kitchen Collander Moll, the housekeeper, was making treacle tarts. She was rolling pastry at one end of the table while, at the other, Odd was helping Elsewhere with his stamp collection. Many people wrote to Fenton House from all over the world and Collander Moll always saved the envelopes for Elsewhere. Now they were tearing off the corners of the envelopes with the stamps and soaking them in saucers of warm water. Gently they peeled each stamp from its bit of envelope and set it to dry with the others before sticking them in the album.

Collander Moll was tugging and pulling at the pastry, kneading the lard and flour and water until it was almost as stretchy as chewing gum. Then she sprinkled the pastry board with flour, slapped the lump down on it and, after flouring the rolling pin, began to roll it backwards and forwards so that the lump of dough oozed out, becoming larger and thinner. When it was thin enough she cut out round shapes for tarts. She paused, looking up at the dusty clock on the mantelpiece.

'There's time for the second post, it is,' she observed. 'Elsewhere, bach! Would you mind going upstairs to see if there's any mail. I'm hoping there's a card from the optician saying my new spectacles are ready. There's blind as a bat I am without them!'

Wiping his hands dry on his trousers, Elsewhere closed the door of the kitchen carefully so as not to make a draught which would have blown all the stamps off the table.

That morning there were many visitors wandering round Fenton House admiring the famous collection of harpsichords and stringed instruments. Elsewhere waved to a young student, a friend of his, who was practising on a clavichord in the dining-room.

On the polished oak table in the hall, where the National Trust brochures and postcards of Fenton House were on sale, and notices about concerts were displayed, he found two letters. One was addressed to Odd. The other envelope read:

Elsewhere took the two letters into the tiny office under the stairs with its window like a port-hole looking out over the green sea of the back lawn. He perched on the high stool by the tall desk, where spare guide books and postcards were stored, and opened his letter. He drew out a thick card printed with gold lettering and read:

TIPPITY HOUSE

His Majesty, the King of the Clowns,
on the eve of his retirement
invites you to a Gathering
at Tippity House upon the occasion
of the Coronation of his successor

Accompanying the invitation was a sheet of note-paper which carried the simple message, in the King's fine copper-plate handwriting:

Dear Elsewhere, the time has come!

Elsewhere took a deep breath and let it out in bits, all wobbly. His hand was shaking. Now that it was really about to happen, and he was to be crowned the next King of the Clowns, he was suddenly very scared.

At that moment he heard soft footsteps padding along the hall.

'Oh, there you are!' said Odd, peering round the

door. 'What are you doing?' Then noticing the expression on Elsewhere's face and the letter in his hand he asked, 'Is it . . .?'

Elsewhere nodded.

'It's come at last!' he said. With a sigh he slid off the stool and handed Odd his own letter.

'Will you open it for me?' said Odd. 'You know my paws aren't very good for opening letters.'

Elsewhere took a similar invitation card out of the envelope and also a letter. The letter read:

TIPPITY HOUSE

Dear Odd,
Welcome to the coronation of our mutual friend. You may let Collander Moll and Hallelujah Jones into the secret.
But no one else.

The two friends raced down the back stairs to tell Collander Moll who had just put the treacle tarts in the oven. She stared at them, her face flushed and damp, as they told her the news.

'A Coronation?' she kept repeating. 'A Coronation? Elsewhere?' Then she added. 'I'll have to mind my P's and Q's now, won't I!' She laughed, wiping her hands on her apron.

'Dad!' she yelled, as she heard Hallelujah coming in for his elevenses. 'Dad! Have you heard the news? Elsewhere's going to be King!'

Hallelujah stared at Elsewhere, then at Odd, and back to Collander Moll, thinking it was some kind of a joke.

'King of the castle, more like!' he grunted. 'Now, where's my tea, girl?'

'Oh, Dad!' exploded Collander Moll. 'It's not every day one of the family becomes royalty, look you, and all you can do is joke! Elsewhere's going to become King of the Clowns!'

'Yes, well, I daresay it will suit him!' sniffed Hallelujah. 'Now, where's that tea?'

'Oh, but Moll, you mustn't tell anyone else yet,' said Odd earnestly. He was afraid she would immediately rush across the road to tell her friend, Mrs Robb, and then down the street, popping into all the shops, telling everyone in Hampstead the news.

'You've got to keep it a secret,' he stressed, 'until the King has told all the clowns at the Gathering.'

But Collander Moll seemed not to be listening.

'Now what shall I wear?' she asked dramatically. 'Oh, Dad!' she went on, turning to Hallelujah, 'If only we'd kept Mam's old wedding dress I could have worn that!'

Odd and Elsewhere looked at each other. They did not like to say that Collander Moll had not been invited, that it was an occasion only for clowns. Odd had been made an honorary clown long ago so it was all right for him.

Collander Moll observed the two friends give each other a look and she frowned.

'It's not like an ordinary coronation,' stammered Odd.

'Perhaps your invitation's in the post,' suggested Elsewhere tactfully.

'And perhaps not!' snapped Collander Moll. 'I know when I'm not wanted!'

With that she bustled out of the room, banging the door behind her. They could hear her stomping upstairs, and they knew she would go and be rude to the visitors, telling them it was closing time even though it was not.

'Oh, dear!' sighed Odd. 'Now we've hurt her feelings.'

'No, you haven't, lad,' replied Hallelujah, his eyes twinkling over the tops of his spectacles. 'She's just

jumped to conclusions, that's all. Been doing it all her life. Result is she's up in the air one minute, and down in the dumps the next. Up and down, down and up, like a see-saw. She's only got to see a telegram and she thinks there's a death in the family. Once she gets an idea in her head, off she goes like a terrier. That's why she's always forgetting things. Brain's like a collander, full of holes!'

He paused, sniffing. He got up suddenly, taking a cloth and opening the oven door. 'Bless my tarnished buttons if she hasn't gone and forgotten your treacle tarts!'

He clattered the tin down on the table. They stared at the dark brown and black shapes.

'Look more like toffee tarts, if you ask me!' chuckled Hallelujah. 'Still, I daresay they'll all go down the red passage once they've cooled.'

'Perhaps we could soak them in water like the stamps,' said Odd wistfully, 'and that would soften them up.'

Hallelujah closed the oven door and put the cloth back on its hook.

'How're you going to get to Tippity House this time?' he asked.

'I think we should take Tipsy and the caravan,' said Elsewhere. Odd looked at him.

'I know what you're thinking,' said Elsewhere, 'but it really won't be like the last time we went travelling together and we nearly had an accident on the motorway.'

'Well then,' said Hallelujah, tapping out his pipe, and becoming businesslike all of a sudden, 'if you two like to give the caravan a good clean out, I'll groom Tipsy and get her ready for the road. And by then Moll will have calmed down and be ready to make up some food for you – *Your Majesty!*' he added with a grin.

The first star in the West was gleaming, and on the curve of the hill every bush, tree and twig was etched in black against the green-blue twilit sky. Slowly, on to the sky-line, as in a shadow play, there travelled the tiny silhouette of a horse and a caravan. Perched on the driver's seat, holding the reins, two small figures could be seen in the light of an oil lamp that shone like a glow worm through the open door.

Odd looked up at the first star and sang:

Twinkle, twinkle, little star,
How I wonder what you are!
Up above the world so high,
Like a diamond in the sky.

When the blazing sun is gone, sang Elsewhere, joining in,
When he nothing shines upon,
Then you show your little light,
Twinkle, twinkle, all the night.

Then the traveller in the dark, sang Odd,

Thanks you for your tiny spark, sang Elsewhere.
He could not see which way to go,
If you did not twinkle so! they sang together.

Odd and Elsewhere had decided to travel by night in order to avoid most of the traffic. Because the autumn nights were cold, Collander Moll had insisted that they wrap up warm. She lent Odd one of her old coats which came right down to the ground, and some thick woollen gloves. He wound his scarf around his neck. Elsewhere wore two knitted scarves, and Hallelujah's old army great-coat. They sat with a rug over their knees and each had a hot water bottle on his lap.

'You'd think we were going to explore the North Pole!' giggled Odd when they had set off. But by the small hours of the morning it was so cold, perched high above Tipsy, that they were glad of the extra warmth.

Although there was almost no traffic at night they were surprised to discover how much other activity there was going on while other people were sleeping. Owls hooted; bats squeaked; in the hedges small birds chirped in their sleep; hedgehogs grunted their way through the long grass; foxes were glimpsed and, once, they saw a badger crossing the road in the moonlight.

Clip, clop; clip, clop; went Tipsy's hooves on the hard surface of the road, while the wooden wheels rumbled and grumbled. It was now the third night of their journey and Elsewhere was holding the reins. Suddenly he spoke.

'It's a funny thing, Odd, but now that I'm about to become King, I can't help feeling that, just at the last minute, something is going to prevent it.'

'But what could go wrong?' asked Odd. He had noticed

that Elsewhere had been very silent for most of the journey.

'I keep thinking how Coco knows he is not going to be King,' replied Elsewhere.

'Well?' said Odd.

Coco was the French clown and very famous. Most of the clowns expected him to be the next King. He was very popular and the most obvious choice.

'Just supposing,' continued Elsewhere, 'that, somehow, Coco has found out that I am going to be King.'

'But how could he?' replied Odd. 'Once the old King has chosen his successor it is kept a secret until the time comes for him to name the new King. That's how it's been for centuries. You know that better than I.'

'But Coco is very special!' argued Elsewhere. 'And the King might have changed his mind!'

'But if the King had done that,' replied Odd patiently, 'he would not have sent you an invitation to your own Coronation!'

'I suppose you are right,' sighed Elsewhere. 'It's probably all these trees. They keep giving me such gloomy thoughts!'

On either side of the road were the tall trees of a wood. There were huge oak trees, and many firs and spruces. The trees grew thickly together, shutting out the moon and stars.

Suddenly a voice rang out sharply on the night air like the crack of a pistol.

'Halt! Stand and deliver!'

There, in the centre of the road, stood a darkened figure, with a scarf over his nose and mouth, and a hat pulled down low over the eyes. In his hand he held what looked like a gun.

'It's a highwayman!' gasped Elsewhere.

'Don't be silly!' laughed Odd. 'You don't get highwaymen today!'

But at that moment a second voice rang out.

'Your carriage or your life!'

This time the voice seemed to come from overhead. Peering up, the two friends could just make out the shape of another masked figure, hanging from the branch of an oak tree.

And now a third voice rang out.

'Stand and deliver!' This voice came from behind the caravan.

'We're surrounded!' gasped Elsewhere.

At that moment the first figure shouted to Elsewhere, 'You there with the reins! Yes, *you*! Drop those reins and get down!'

Elsewhere hissed to Odd. 'It's a plot. I know it is! They're after *me*, don't you see? I told you I had a feeling something like this was going to happen. You can tell by their accent they are foreigners. Coco's hired them to kidnap me!'

There was a thump, and the caravan shuddered, as the second figure leapt on to the roof. Tipsy whinnied and Elsewhere pulled hard on the reins. The first man grabbed hold of Tipsy, while the third man leapt on to the driving board.

It was then that Tipsy decided to ignore the reins. Quite suddenly she bolted forward. Elsewhere at once slackened the reins and allowed her to have her head. Handing the reins to Odd, he turned to grapple with the three men, as the wheels of the caravan spun faster and faster.

To his surprise the three highwaymen had removed their masks and were roaring with laughter. They were laughing so much that they nearly fell off the caravan. At that moment the road began to wind uphill and the caravan slowed down.

Odd and Elsewhere stared at the three figures who were roaring with laughter.

'It's *them*! It's *them*! It's Odd and Elsewhere!' they kept saying.

And Odd and Elsewhere exclaimed, 'Why, it's not

kidnappers at all. It's . . . . .'

And the first figure shouted, *'Whizz!'*

And the second figure shouted, *'Phizz!'*

And the third shouted, *'Tizz!'*

And with that, the German clowns, Whizz, Phizz and Tizz, who were Elsewhere's especial friends, shook hands with Odd and Elsewhere, and threw away the bits of stick they had used as revolvers.

'But why on earth did you think we were kidnappers?' asked Whizz.

'And why did *you* pretend you were highwaymen?' countered Elsewhere.

'Well,' replied Whizz, 'when we got our invitation for the Coronation. . . .'

'By the way,' interrupted Phizz, 'have you any idea who's going to be the new King?'

'Perhaps it's going to be Elsewhere!' laughed Tizz.

Elsewhere busied himself helping Odd make a pot of tea for their friends and pretended not to hear.

'*Anyway!*' continued Whizz, 'we set off at once and didn't have any difficulty hitch-hiking as far as Calais. It was once we landed in England that we ran into difficulties. People just didn't seem to want to give us lifts. Perhaps they were nervous of picking up three people. And so. . . .'

'As we were getting desperate,' continued Phizz,

'We decided,' concluded Tizz, 'to hold up the very next car, vehicle, carriage or conveyance, that came along. Little did we think it would be you!'

'It's funny,' remarked Whizz, sipping his tea, 'but we haven't seen any of the others. Not like last time there was a Gathering. Of course I expect a lot will be flying in. Especially the American and the Japanese clowns.'

'I wonder if Coco will use his own private plane?' said Phizz.

'I expect so,' answered Tizz.

As his friends continued chatting Elsewhere sat silent, thinking.

He was wondering how Coco would react when he learned that it was he, Elsewhere, who was to be the next King of the Clowns. Coco was a great artist. There was no doubt about that. Even Elsewhere had thought he ought to be King. Yet the King had chosen Elsewhere.

There was a silence and Elsewhere was aware that the others were looking at him.

'Cheer up, Elsewhere!' they shouted. 'You're not going to be King!'

And roaring with laughter, Whizz, Phizz and Tizz set off with Odd and Elsewhere on the last stage of their journey.

Moisture dripped from the bare trees, and cattle were breathing out small clouds of mist. The sky was grey and green.

'Looks like snow!' shivered Odd. 'I hope they've got a good fire burning when we get there.'

'If it snows,' laughed Whizz, 'we'll turn into snow-men!'

'And *then*,' added Phizz, 'we'll have to thaw out when we get there.'

'Of course, we might melt away altogether!' sniffed Tizz who had caught a cold. His nose was running so much that he kept hoping it would freeze into an icicle.

As they turned into the long drive that led up through parkland to Tippity House, the home of the King, Elsewhere remarked, 'That's funny!'

'What is?' asked Odd, who was making a drink of lemon and honey for Tizz's cold.

'Well, there doesn't seem to be anyone about,' replied Elsewhere. 'Not like the last time. Do you remember? All the windows were crowded with clowns leaning out to wave and cheer?'

'Yes, and the King was standing at the top of the steps to welcome everyone as they arrived!' added Whizz.

'Perhaps the Gathering's been cancelled,' said Elsewhere anxiously.

'Mind you, it is winter time now, 'observed Phizz. 'So you'd hardly expect the windows to be open and people leaning out.'

'And there is smoke coming from the chimney,' remarked Odd.

'And where there's smoke there's fire,' added Phizz.

'Oh, good!' cried Tizz, blowing his streaming nose.

They were halfway up the long drive when they saw the small aeroplane on an open stretch of parkland in front of the large red-brick house with its many windows. They could see the colours of the French flag painted on the fuselage, and they knew at once that it was Coco's plane.

'I wonder what that means?' whispered Elsewhere anxiously to Odd. 'Do you think the King has changed his mind and sent especially for Coco? There's no sign of any other carriages or cars or wagons, and perhaps that's why we haven't met anyone else on the way.'

Above them, perched on the roof of the caravan, Whizz, Phizz and Tizz were singing the French national anthem –

Marchons! Marchons! Auz armes, citoyens!

'But all the other vehicles,' replied Odd, 'would be round at the back where the garages and stables are. Don't worry.'

And indeed, when they drove round to the back of the house, they found a special car-park had been made to accommodate the hundreds of vehicles in which all the other clowns had travelled. And inside Tippity House the great hall was packed with clowns who all that day and the day before had been arriving from Sweden, Denmark, Finland, Norway, Russia, Japan, America, Brazil, Sierra Leone, Mexico, the Seychelles, Jamaica, Uruguay, Australia, New Zealand and many other places.

The king was seated in a high chair in front of a blazing fire at the far end of the hall. He seemed much older than when they had last seen him. Odd was puzzled at first until he realised he was not wearing his clown's make-up. One grey eye-brow sagged.

'You must forgive my not being on the steps to greet you,' he said, 'but I've not been at all well of late, and these icy North winds are none too good for my old bones.'

He asked after Collander Moll and Hallelujah Jones and their other friends, and was pleased to hear that Odd and Elsewhere had travelled in the caravan which he had given them one Christmas. Then he turned to a tall elegant clown by his side and said, 'You know Coco, don't you?'

Coco stepped forward with a flourish to shake hands with Elsewhere.

'Enchanté de vous voir de nouveau, Monsieur Not-Here!' he said.

'Elsewhere!' corrected Odd.

'Oh, pardon mille fois!' purred Coco. 'Monsieur *Else*-where!'

He then turned to Odd and bowed. 'Et vous, mon petit ami singulier, Monsieur Odd!' He looked round at the assembled company and added with a smile, 'Messieurs Odd et Elsewhere, les inséparables.'

Everyone laughed and thought how witty Coco was, but Odd did not think so at all. He thought he was just being clever and making fun of Elsewhere. He did not mind for himself; after all, if you had a name like his you expected people to make stupid jokes like 'Oh, how odd!' or 'Aren't you odd!'

Suddenly there was a loud sneeze, *Atchoo*! from Tizz.

'Have a tissue!' said Phizz, handing him a paper handkerchief.

'Oh, please, may I take Tizz up to his room?' asked Odd of the King. 'I think he ought to be in bed. He has a dreadful cold.'

'But I don't want to go to bed!' replied Tizz stubbornly. 'I don't want to miss all the fun!' He blew his nose very loudly into the paper handkerchief.

Whizz and Phizz ran round handing out paper handkerchiefs to all the other clowns.

'Right!' announced Whizz. 'When I say, Sneeze! I want everyone to blow his nose. Ready, steady – *sneeze!*'

At once there was such a blowing and a trumpeting,
a sneezing and a sniffing,
a whooping and a wheezing,
a huffing and a puffing,
a sniffling and a snorting,
a spluttering and a swooshing,
that it seemed as though the whole house were exploding.

'And again!' called Whizz. 'Ready, steady – A-WHIZZ-OO!'

'And again!' called Phizz. 'Ready, steady – A-PHIZZ-OO!'

'And again!' laughed Tizz. 'Ready, steady – A-TIZZ-OO!'

There was a pause and everyone looked clear eyed and more wide awake.

'How you feeling, Tizz?' asked Whizz brightly.

'I'm fine!' laughed Tizz, without any sound of a cold at all.

'Good!' replied Whizz. 'I think that's got rid of all the germs here for a while.' He grinned. 'An old Bavarian cure for the common cold!' he explained.

Suddenly there was a loud banging at the door and a ringing of many small bells, a delicate sound like a xylophone. The door opened and there entered a boy with bright red cheeks, dressed in a jacket and knickerbockers, with a satchel slung over his chest. With him was a girl, also with red cheeks, and wearing a long dress and a mob cap. She looked like a younger Collander Moll.

'Why, it's Wiggee and Bloggs!' exclaimed Elsewhere in delight. Bloggs blushed and curtseyed while Wiggee slapped Elsewhere on the back.

'Well,' laughed the King, 'you couldn't have a Gathering without Bloggs' famous Tippity Pudding, now could you? And Wiggee, of course, to look after the horses.'

Once again, through the open door, there came a carillon of tiny bells, chinking, clinking, tinkling, chiming and jingling.

'What is that tin-tin-abulation?' asked the King.

Odd pricked up his ears at the sound of this word. He had never heard such a beautiful word to describe the sound of ringing Bells.

'Oh, Gummy!' gasped Wiggee. 'I did tell them to come in, but they're very shy. It's the Chinese contingent. Bloggs and I gave them a lift in our cart.'

'Ask them in!' said the King. 'Don't leave them standing outside on the doorstep. What will they think of us?'

Into the hall entered twelve Chinese clowns who clicked their heels and bowed before the King. In their hands they held silver hoops from which were suspended many small bells of varying sizes. These they tipped and tilted as they moved, so making the tintinabulation that had been heard earlier. Ringing their handbells they now sang a little song.

Ching-a-ring-a-ring-ching! Crinkum-Crankum!
What a crop of chop sticks, hongs and gongs!
Hundred thousand Chinese lanterns,
Hung among the bells and ding-dongs!
We are come to greet you, meet you,
Ching-a-ring-a-ring-ching, crinkum-crankum!

The King replied with a speech welcoming them and thanking them for having come such a long way. He then invited everyone to do whatever they liked until dinner time after which, he said, he would be naming his successor.

As on many occasions in the past the long table in the great hall of Tippity House was laid for a splendid banquet. Each course was prepared from a different national recipe and on this occasion, in honour of the Chinese, there was bird's nest soup.

'I don't think I quite like the sound of that!' murmured Odd to Elsewhere as they took their places at the table.

The King was dressed in his full costume and his face made up in the traditional clown's mask so that now he looked exactly as Odd and Elsewhere remembered first seeing him.

There was much chattering and laughter as dish followed dish, and finally Bloggs appeared with her Tippity Pudding. It was so famous that she always had to be sure and make enough for two helpings all round.

'Bloggs!' smiled the King. 'You have surpassed yourself, if that is possible!' And Bloggs, giggling with delight, dropped a curtsey and also very nearly dropped the empty bowl.

At long last the King rose to make his speech.

Looking around him, Odd could sense the excitement in the air. The flames of the candles, set in candelabra all down the centre of the table, seemed to stretch higher, while the huge logs on the fire hissed and cracked like fireworks.

'Friends and fellow artists,' began the King. 'We are met here in the house of Grimaldi on the occasion of my retirement and the coronation of your new King. It is therefore appropriate to say something about Joseph Grimaldi, the greatest of English clowns and to recall for you his final performance at Covent Garden Opera House in London on Friday June 27th 1828, when he made, as I do now, his farewell address.

'"Ladies and gentlemen," Grimaldi said on that occasion, "I appear before you now for the last time. I need not assure you of the sad regret with which I say it, but sickness and infirmity have come upon me, and I can no longer wear the motley. I have jumped my last jump,

played my last trick, cracked my last joke. I cannot describe the pleasure I felt tonight in once more assuming my cap and bells, that dress in which I have so often been made happy in your applause. Ladies and gentlemen, I must hasten to bid you farewell, but the pain I feel in doing so is lessened by seeing before me the disproof of the old saying that favourites have no friends. Ladies and gentlemen, may you and yours enjoy the blessing of health is the fervent prayer of Joseph Grimaldi. Farewell! Farewell!"'

The King paused. It was, thought Odd, almost as though Grimaldi's farewell speech had become his own.

'At the end,' continued the King, 'Grimaldi stood on the stage, swaying before the footlights, tears running down his cheeks as the audience roared their applause, thundering the floor with their feet, banging the benches and throwing their hats into the air. Wave after wave of

applause exploded from the thousands of people who wanted to express their gratitude to the man who, for so many years, had given them so much happiness and gaiety.

'The streets outside were thronged with people waiting to see him come out and, as he entered his coach which stood at the stage door, they gave him three cheers. Hundreds followed the carriage until it reached his house and, upon being helped out, he was once again hailed by shouts of "Joey! Good old Joey! Joey the clown!"'

Lifting his glass, the King turned to the portrait of Grimaldi on the wall behind him, and looking up at that plump laughing face with the bushy eyebrows, sparkling eyes and full lips, said, 'Friends, let us now drink to the greatest of all English clowns. I give you, *Joseph. . . .*'

Rising, and raising their glasses towards the portrait, the clowns shouted the answer to this, their password, '*Grimaldi!*'

Then they all sat down to refill their glasses and to listen to the most important part of the King's speech when, as they knew, he would announce who was to succeed him.

'My friends, perhaps the hardest of the many tasks that a King has to face is that of choosing his own successor. How does he decide to select that clown whom he considers to be worthy as a successor to the great Grimaldi?

'Joey the Clown, as you all know, was an acrobat, a juggler, a swordsman, a dancer, a singer, a mime. He could design and paint scenery, make props, arrange stage fights, and choreograph dances. He also loved to garden, make shoes, do carpentry, invent conjuring tricks, play the violin, keep pigeons, and collect butterflies.

'Therefore he who would be King of the Clowns must be a master not only of his own particular craft but of all aspects of circus life. Indeed, every clown must be able to turn his hand to anything, whether it be to replace the lion-tamer or the magician, sell tickets in the box office, or sweep up after the performance.

'In spite of his success, however, Grimaldi experienced many difficulties and disappointments. When his London home was burgled, and his prize collection of butterflies was stolen – to this day it has never been found – Grimaldi was to experience the first of many losses. He was to lose his wife, his son, his beloved garden, his pigeons, and be forced, through ill health, to retire early from the stage. At the end he was completely alone, and his limbs so crippled that he had to be carried on the shoulders of a friend whenever he went out.

'In the same way,' continued the King, 'he who would be King must know what it is to be top of the bill and what it is to be neglected. He must know what it is to have everything and what it is to have nothing. For the King must never be deceived by power. He has power only so long as he is King and he must use it well on behalf of you all.'

The King paused. There was silence in the great hall of Tippity House. Even the logs had burned down to a bed of glowing ash; the candles, too, along the table had burned low, their flames wobbling in the draughts of the old house. Odd gazed round at the faces now turned expectantly towards the King. He looked across the table at Coco whose black eyes glittered in his white face.

'Many of you are famous in your own countries as well as throughout the world,' continued the King. 'But there is only one among you who has known what it is to be famous and what it is to be forgotten. There was a time when he was the most famous trapeze artist in the world yet few now remember his name. He is the one who is closest to the image and the ideal of our great hero, Joseph Grimaldi. He is also, I hope, one who will bring back to these shores the great tradition of clowning which for so long has been lost.

'My friends and fellow artists, I bid you stand with me to pay homage to my successor – Elsewhere!'

The choice of Elsewhere as the next King of the Clowns took many by surprise, so convinced had they been that Coco would be the one chosen. Odd noticed how those closest to Coco, and who always followed him wherever he went, raised their eyebrows in surprise when the King made his announcement, but Coco's face betrayed no emotion.

The silence seemed to Odd to last for ever although it was only a few seconds, during which Elsewhere stood quite still, his face very pale.

It was Coco who broke the silence. He rose to his feet and at once everyone rose with him.

'Three cheers for Elsewhere!' he called.

And then everyone was crowding up to Elsewhere to congratulate him, after which they broke up into small groups in different parts of the hall, buzzing like many swarms of bees.

The King said goodnight and announced that he was retiring early to bed.

'Tomorrow,' he said to Elsewhere,' we will meet after breakfast to discuss details of the coronation ceremony, and there will be a rehearsal in the afternoon, to make sure everything is in order for the event itself the following day.'

During all this Odd kept in the background. Clowns from different parts of the world were wanting to acquaint themselves with the King-to-be and were lining up to speak with Elsewhere. As Odd ambled about the hall, his paws clasped behind his back, he felt a little out of it all because he was only an honorary clown. As he wandered from group to group he could not help overhearing bits of conversation.

'After all,' an elderly clown was saying, 'the King himself was an outsider when he was elected. No one had heard of him at the time. Yet look what a wise King he has been. I'd trust his judgement any day.'

Another group buzzed more angrily. A large pompous clown was saying in a booming voice, 'If you want my opinion. . . .'

'But we don't!' chorused others in the group.

'If you want my opinion,' continued the pompous clown as though he had not been interrupted, 'the King's gone ga-ga! He must be out of his mind. I mean, what do we know about this clown? A mere has-been!'

At this point a perky little Peruvian clown who always nodded in agreement with everything the pompous clown said, interrupted to add, 'Yes, do you remember? It must have been at the last Gathering, he made an awful mess of his first turn in the ring!'

'Yes, I remember that,' replied another clown, 'but you must admit he was better the second time round.'

'Oh, I grant you he's good on the trapeze,' replied the pompous clown. 'But do you know what saved his act that time? If you want my opinion. . . .'

'Oh, but we don't!' chorused the same group.

'If you want my opinion,' continued the pompous clown, exactly as though he had not been interrupted, 'what saved his act that second time was that bear, his friend, what's his name?'

'Odd!' prompted the perky little Peruvian clown.

'Yes, Odd! If it hadn't been for his presence of mind, as I recall, and his determination to see his friend make a go of it, the act would have been an absolute fiasco!'

'Oh, come now, I think you're being a little unfair!' challenged another clown. 'We hadn't seen work on the trapeze to equal that for a very long time. You could tell by the applause at the end. Everyone was in agreement. And I think. . . .' Suddenly the clown who was speaking broke off as he noticed Odd approaching, and they began to talk about the weather instead.

Odd felt rather sad and lonely. He sensed that they were now shy of him because he was a close friend of the King-to-be. Also, Elsewhere seemed suddenly removed from him and he began to realise that from now on he

would probably see less of him, especially once he had become King and started travelling about the world.

Odd wandered into the library. There, in front of the window, he found the King looking out at the night sky.

'So you haven't gone to bed yet?' said Odd.

'Hullo, Odd!' replied the King, smiling. 'I was looking up at your constellation, the little Bear. He's very clear tonight. And I was thinking that it is the Little Bear who carries the North Star that guides men on their long journeys across seas and across deserts. And you have been a kind of North Star to Elsewhere!'

Odd gazed up into the old, worn face of the King and thought: He reminds me of someone. Who is it? And then he realised. It was of his friend, the Great Bear. Perhaps, thought Odd, the King was to Elsewhere what the Great Bear was to him.

At that moment Elsewhere entered the library, looking very thoughtful. The King seemed to sense what he was thinking for he said, 'Don't let all that argy-bargy out there worry you, Elsewhere. Nor you, Odd,' he added. 'They are bound to be surprised. There are bound to be a lot of hurt feelings and disappointed ambitions. Not everybody can be king! It was the same when I was elected. You could hear them talking up and down the corridors, late into the night, and they held secret meetings in each others' rooms. It was like the buzzing of a lot of angry wasps. But it's better for them to have it out now. You'll find that, come the Coronation, once you are actually King, they'll be unswerving in their loyalty. And Elsewhere will be a good king,' he added, turning to Odd. 'They can't see that yet as I can. But at the right time Elsewhere will come into his own as King. You will see!'

For a while, the King, Odd and Elsewhere, sat in front of the fire, watching the sparks fly up the chimney.

'And what will you do now?' asked Odd.

The King chuckled. 'At this moment I am going to bed. Tonight I am just a little tired and empty. It's like when you give a performance in the ring or on the stage – Elsewhere will tell you the same – you are just that little less yourself. You have given away something of yourself and that's why there is this empty feeling.'

He gazed into the fire and added quietly, almost to himself, 'The sparks fly up but the fire itself is dying out!'

Then he grinned broadly at them both, as he got up to go. 'I'm going to my caravan and if, just before you go to bed, you lean out of your window, you will hear me snoring!'

After the King had gone, Odd and Elsewhere sat on in front of the fire. Elsewhere sighed.

'I've got to do something special,' he said. 'Something

so special that they'll all see that I'm going to be a King Extra-Ordinary!'

Odd looked up. He could see the tremendous determination in Elsewhere's face and he knew that once he made up his mind to do something nothing would stop him.

'Coco and his friends think I'm a nonentity,' continued Elsewhere. 'Well, I shall show them. Do you know what I am going to do?'

Odd shook his head.

'I'm going to find Grimaldi's butterfly collection and present it to Tippity House where it rightly belongs!'

Odd clapped his paws. 'Oh, that would be exciting!' he cried. 'But how will you go about it?'

'I don't know yet,' replied Elsewhere. 'And it will take time. But I shall make a start at Grimaldi's old house in London. It must be somewhere and I'm going to search and search until I find it! When I was listening to the King talking about Grimaldi and he told us about Grimaldi's butterflies, I had a feeling then that somehow I was meant to find them.'

He got up. Suddenly he seemed more cheerful and more sure of himself. 'I think I'll go to bed now,' he said. 'It's going to be a busy two days. Goodnight, Odd!'

Odd was beginning to feel sleepy himself. Then he remembered his new word, *Tin-tin-abulation* and he murmured it over and over to himself, like a magic charm. . . .

When he awoke the room was in darkness and the fire had gone out. Only a glimmer of ashes remained. Close by he could hear voices whispering, as though they did not want to be overheard. Something told him to stay where he was, hidden in the shadowy recess of the big wing chair.

'But, Coco, you must do something!' urged a husky voice. 'You can't just stand by and let it happen.'

Odd heard the soft, velvety voice of Coco reply, 'But only le roi, the King, can choose his successor. The King has chosen. Voilà, c'est tout!'

Odd could almost see the shrug of his shoulders, the outstretched elegant hands and the proud cynical smile.

'Mais ce n'est pas tout, mon ami!' answered the first voice. 'That is not all, my friend. The King must change his mind!'

'Mais comment? How is that possible?' demanded Coco impatiently.

'Le voici, here is how!. . . ' answered the husky voice, moving away so that Odd could no longer hear what was being said. In a few moments the conspirators had left the room.

Very thoughtfully Odd climbed the wooden staircase to his room. He wondered if he should tell Elsewhere what he had overheard. But when he popped his head round the door of his friend's room, he saw that he was asleep, his pale cheeks flushed, and his yellow hair splashed across the pillow. Softly he closed the door and went to his own room. After all, the King had told them not to worry.

The King awoke and was conscious that something was different. He lay as though drugged, unable at first to move his limbs. Then he knew what it was. The caravan was on the move! Branches whipped savagely at the sides, and he could hear twigs cracking beneath the hooves of the horse which had been harnessed to the shafts of the caravan. He could hear voices shouting and cursing at the horse to get a move on.

Slowly he sat up and dangled his legs from his bunk at the far end of the caravan, facing the door. He sat there for a while, getting his bearings in the dark, and trying to understand what could have happened. Slowly he moved his way forward, past the stove which was still warm, and past the dresser where he could hear his best china rattling, until he reached the door of the caravan. He turned the handle and pushed. It was locked!

It was then that he realised he had been kidnapped. But why? And by whom?

There was a loud *Whoa*! and the caravan came abruptly to a standstill. The door was unlocked and there, standing on the steps, holding a lantern was . . . Coco!

Gradually it dawned on everyone at Tippity House that the King was nowhere to be found, and when it was reported that his caravan was missing, all the clowns gathered in the great hall to discuss what this could mean.

Whiz, Phizz, and Tizz burst into the hall saying, 'Has anyone seen Coco?'

There was a general murmur of surprise. Not one of them could recall having seen him since the previous evening. Then, as they took a close count, they discovered that the small band of clowns who always followed him everywhere had also vanished.

It was only then that Odd, who had not yet woken up properly, remembered the conversation he had overheard. Now he stumbled out the story, feeling guilty that he had not remembered sooner. There was a hushed silence when he finished. Instinctively everyone turned to Elsewhere as leader, awaiting his comment.

'It looks to me,' he observed, 'as though the King may have been kidnapped. But why?'

'To prevent your Coronation, that's why!' answered Whizz. 'Everyone knows Coco's friends took it for granted he would be King. And there are plenty here who think likewise although they haven't the guts to admit it to your face!'

There was an embarrassed silence.

'But how will kidnapping the King help Coco?' asked Odd.

'If you want my opinion,' ventured the pompous clown, and this time no one chimed in to say they did not, they were all too worried, 'Coco obviously hopes to persuade the King to change his mind. Only the King can name his own successor. Goodness only knows what they may do to him to get their way. If you want my opinion I think the whole system of electing the King in this antiquated Royalist fashion is long overdue for reform. If I had my way . . .'

'All right! All right!' chorused Whizz, Phizz and Tizz. 'We all know what you would do, but this is no time for suggesting electoral reforms! Instead of standing around talking we ought to be making a plan to rescue the King. And since the King has named Elsewhere as his successor, it is for us to do whatever Elsewhere suggests.'

'Hear! Hear!' shouted the other clowns. But before Elsewhere could say anything, one of the youngest, a small boy named Joey, came running in excitedly, red in the face, and out of breath. Odd recognised him as the clown who had first brought him the news that he had been made an honorary clown.

'They've-taken-the-King-to-Brockland-Forest!' he stammered, the words tumbling into one another and tripping over. 'I followed the tracks of the caravan on my bicycle. But I didn't dare go into the Forest because . . . because. . . .'

'That's all right, Joey!' said one of the older clowns

kindly. Most of them knew the stories about Brockland Forest which was centuries old and spread for thousands of acres. You could get lost in there and never come out. At night it was full of strange shapes that sighed and creaked and rustled. It was believed that Merlin, the Welsh wizard, had once lived there.

'Brockland Forest?' said Odd, turning excitedly to Elsewhere. 'But that's where the Great Bear lives now, in Merlin's old chapel!'

All the clowns turned to look at Odd with renewed interest. Not all of them knew the story of the Great Bear, nor of Odd's connection with him, but they had all heard of Merlin, the Welsh wizard. Not for nothing, they were beginning to realise, had the King made this small bear one of them.

'If only we could get a message to the Great Bear I'm sure he can help us!' added Odd.

'I really don't see how a bear can help us in this instance!' protested the pompous clown. 'It would be more to the point if. . . .'

'Please!' interrupted Elsewhere. He turned to the small clown. 'Joey,' he said, 'you've done best of all of us. You did something practical, and I'm proud of you!'

Joey blushed red and beamed with pleasure at this praise.

'Odd and I will take our caravan,' continued Elsewhere, 'and follow their tracks into the Forest. Once we have caught up with them and found their hideaway, we can make our plans, I have no doubt then we shall be glad of the Great Bear's assistance. Joey!'

'Yes, sir?'

'We shall need you to accompany us as far as the edge of the Forest. Once there we'll soon pick up the tracks.'

'I don't think you have much hope of that!' said Whizz. 'Have you noticed the weather?'

While they had been talking, the great hall had gradually darkened. Turning now to look out of the windows they saw that the sky was heavy with snow. Large flakes were drifting slowly down, and already over the lawns and parkland lay a fine layer of white, while the view beyond was curtained by faster falling snow.

'There's no time to be lost!' said Elsewhere briskly.

'But oughtn't some of us to come with you?' asked the pompous clown.

Elsewhere paused briefly and then replied, 'No, it's my place to go. And I need Odd if the Great Bear is to be contacted. But no one else.' He turned to the pompous clown and added, thereby winning a friend for life, 'But I'd like you to be in charge while I'm gone. We'll need a look-out on the roof, and someone to be on duty by the telephone. Check all vehicles are ready to turn out.'

Everything began to move very fast. Wiggee got Tipsy out of the stables and harnessed her up to the caravan. Bloggs, perspiring, came rushing in with a thermos flask of hot coffee and packages of sandwiches. Someone lent them anoraks and wellingtons. And without any more to do, Odd and Elsewhere and Joey set off in the direction of Brockland Forest, while the other clowns huddled anxiously on the front steps in the falling snow in order to give them a rousing cheer.

'It's like Scott and the Antarctic!' murmured Tizz, shivering.

Inside the Forest, where the trees grew to a height of forty feet or more, the snow had already begun to penetrate, drifting down on the dead leaves like sugar on cornflakes. Each bough and branch was ridged with a white fur.

At first, after saying goodbye to Joey, Odd and Elsewhere had found it fairly easy to follow the tracks of the King's caravan as it was apparent that Coco was keeping to a well worn path into the Forest. But as the path began to divide and sub-divide into other paths, leading deeper and deeper into the Forest, they soon became confused and lost.

They were struggling uphill, Tipsy slipping and stumbling, Elsewhere walking beside her, holding the reins, when suddenly the back wheels stuck deep in a rut. Odd placed dead branches behind the wheels as Elsewhere jumped on the driver's seat and tugged at the reins, urging Tipsy to pull really hard. But the back wheels only spun round, slithering in the mud and the snow which spurted all over Odd's face and front as he tried to push the caravan.

'Let me have a try!' said Elsewhere, 'and you take the reins.'

But the result was the same, the back wheels only sunk deeper into the mud and snow. And now, to add to their problems, it was getting dark. They could hear owls hooting and a distant cawing of rooks and then another sound.

'Listen!' said Odd. 'That was a dog barking!'

'It seems to be coming from in front of us,' observed Elsewhere.

'It must mean there is a farm nearby,' said Odd. 'In which case we can get help.'

'We'd better light the lamp inside the caravan,' suggested Elsewhere, 'so we can find our way back easily. We'll take a lantern with us.'

'I'll just give Tipsy some oats first,' called Odd cheerfully, as he hung the feeding bag around her neck.

Slowly they trudged up the track which widened into a lane leading out of the Forest. Ahead of them they

could see, through the driving snow, the blurred lights of a farmhouse on the opposite side of the valley. They could also hear the roar of water.

'It's a river!' cried Odd in dismay. 'How shall we cross it?'

'There must be a bridge,' replied Elsewhere. 'After all, this track wouldn't lead straight towards a river unless there were some way of getting across it.'

But when they reached the banks of the river there was no sign of a bridge.

'What do we do now?' shouted Odd, shivering. Now that they were out of the Forest they were exposed to the full blast of the snow storm, while the noise of the racing water made it difficult to hear each other.

'Just a minute!' called Elsewhere. 'There seems to be something here.'

Odd hurried over to where Elsewhere was holding up the lantern. Beneath the snow they could make out the shape of a concrete platform that carried the pathway across the river. But the level of the river had risen so much that the rest of the bridge was under water.

'I think we'll be all right,' said Elsewhere. 'If we keep to the centre.'

Holding the lantern high, Elsewhere grasped Odd firmly by the paw, and slowly they waded into the icy cold river. The water reached as high as Elsewhere's waist and as high as Odd's chest, and the current was so strong that it kept trying to push them over the edge of the concrete bridge. But at last they were out on the other side and scrambling up the opposite slope to the farm. Now they could hear the putt-putt-putt of a generator.

Reaching the backdoor they banged loudly in case

they should not be heard through the noise of the storm. Someone opened the door and the next moment the two friends were in a large warm kitchen, with damp patches on the walls and a Welsh dresser filled with brightly sparkling blue and white plates. Gathered round the table, having tea with their mother, were several children. A radio blared out the news, and a television set was flickering in one corner. In front of the blazing fire were two figures. One, seated in a high settle, had his back to them; the other, a cheerful, red-faced farmer, was bouncing a bawling baby up and down on his knees, and singing, *Hands, knees, and boomps-a-daisy!*

As the two friends stumbled in, splashed with mud

from head to foot, with epaulettes of snow on their shoulders, quickly forming puddles at their feet, the farmer stopped singing and turned down the sound on the television, while the farmer's wife switched off the radio.

'We are very sorry to disturb you,' apologised Elsewhere in the sudden silence, while all the children stared at the two strange figures who had stumbled so suddenly out of the night into their kitchen. 'We got lost and our caravan stuck in the mud and we heard your dog barking and we walked through the river and, and... *Atchoo*!'

As Elsewhere sneezed loudly, the large figure who had been seated in the settle rose and growled. 'It's one of those tinkers I was telling you about!'

Odd stared up at the tall figure with the hairy face and spectacles glinting in the firelight and he cried out, 'Oh, Great Bear, it's you!'

All at once he knew where they were. They were with friends. They were in the kitchen of Farmer Thomas and his family who had helped Odd when he first came to find the Great Bear.

'Goodness bless my soul and give me peace!' exclaimed the Great Bear.' But it's Ursus Minor, the Little Bear! Welcome, my little one! But what on earth brings you here on a night like this, and with this – this *tinker?*'

'He's not a tinker!' Odd protested indignantly. 'He's Elsewhere. He's my friend. *You* know!'

Mrs Thomas was fussing and clucking like an anxious hen. A tin bath was pulled out in front of the fire and filled with saucepans of hot water; dry clothes were found; and hot food placed on the table; while the children crowded round the two friends.

'Will you loop the loop for us after supper?' croaked Stephen, the youngest.

'And leap through a wooden hoop?' added Jane.

'And dive in a tub of water?' said Andrew.

'Are you a famous clown?' asked Jane. 'Really really famous?' Odd was just about to reply and say that Elsewhere was going to be the *King* of the Clowns when Mrs Thomas shooed them all out of the room and up to bed.

'I can't hear myself think with all that noise!' she said.

Sitting at the table, eating steak and kidney pie, Odd looked up at the Great Bear and asked, 'Why did you think Elsewhere was a tinker?'

'Because,' replied the Great Bear,' earlier today in the Forest, I came across a bunch of ruffians, dressed like Elsewhere, who looked to me exactly like tinkers. They didn't see me because I kept in the background and so overheard what they were saying. They had lost their way in the Forest, couldn't get the stove to burn because all the wood around was wet, and they kept referring to someone inside the caravan, whom I couldn't see, as the King. I've never met a more damp, miserable looking lot of ruffians in my life. They were obviously up to no good, so I came to tell my good friend Farmer Thomas here about them, in case they were after stealing his chickens. Their leader seemed to be someone called Chocolate. . . .'

'You mean *Coco*!' laughed Odd.

'Oh, do I?' replied the Great Bear. Then he paused, peering over his spectacles, and added, 'How do you know that?'

'Because that's who we have been trying to track down,' explained Elsewhere. 'And we need to find him as soon as we can!'

Farmer Thomas and his brother Dai, followed by the Great Bear and Odd and Elsewhere, made their way to a huge new barn at the back of the farm.

'We've had this built since you were last here!' shouted Farmer Thomas to Odd above the noise of the wind. He unlocked a padlock and slid away a section of the wall, revealing a space inside like an aeroplane hangar. He pressed several switches and bars of lighting flickered on overhead. The lofty space was stacked high with hay on one side while on the other, in separate pens, were cattle. In one stall was a cow with a newborn calf; in another stood a bull; in a third were curly headed bullocks lying in hay. Everything was silent, musty with the smell of hay, the animals staring dumbly as though hypnotised by the light. At one end of the building were farm wagons, a station wagon, and several tractors. Farmer Thomas collected ropes and chains for rescuing Odd and Elsewhere's caravan, as well as spades in case they had to dig it out of the snow. He also handed each of them a torch.

. . . . .

The headlights lit up the river as they drove through the swirling water, and the snowflakes, falling slowly now, glistened in the light. As they entered the Forest, branches cracked and snapped.

Whoo-ooo! A barn owl flew softly above them and Odd, looking up through the falling breadcrumbs of snow, recognised it as Taliesin, Merlin's Messenger, who lived in the Forest with the Great Bear.

At last, ahead of them, they could see their caravan, banked with snow, and Tipsy covered with a white coat and with a white mane. Mist was rising from her nostrils and she whinnied as they approached. Quickly Dai Thomas unharnessed her, while the others dug out the caravan. Farmer Thomas switched on a small spotlight attached to his tractor so that they could see more clearly what they were doing. He turned his tractor around and fastened chains from the back of it to the front of the caravan, while Dai attached more chains

from the rear of the caravan to his tractor. In this way, when they moved off, as Farmer Thomas hauled the caravan, Dai's tractor following behind was able to prevent the caravan rolling downhill and crashing into his brother's tractor in front. Slowly the caravan was pulled out of the gulping, sucking mud and snow, while Elsewhere followed on foot, leading Tipsy by the reins. Once the caravan had been parked inside the new barn, Mrs Thomas gave Tipsy a good rub down and put her in a stall with plenty of hay and oats. The rest set off once again on the two tractors, in search of the King's caravan and Coco's gang.

Hour after hour they drove. Taliesin flew ahead, leading the way, guiding them through a maze of trees which seemed to grow taller and more closely together the deeper they journeyed into the Forest. By now it was beginning to freeze, powdering the snow into tiny crystals which winked and twinkled in the light from

the headlamps. Taliesin flew always just within the beam of light, like a large moth.

It was when Taliesin hooted and perched on the branch of a tree that the Great Bear gave the signal for them to stop. Elsewhere then turned to speak to the others.

'The Great Bear says that the King's caravan is about two miles from here. We must leave the vehicles and make the rest of the journey on foot otherwise they will hear us coming. Now when we get there. . . .'

They gathered round in a close group while Elsewhere outlined his plan to them. At one point the Great Bear chuckled.

'We'll have to do without torches,' concluded Elsewhere. 'Taliesin will guide us with hoots. Great Bear, will you lead the way?'

Linking hands, or paws, they followed the Great Bear whose keen sense of smell was sufficient to guide him. It was so dark that it was like being blindfold. They had to tread softly in order to avoid making the snow crunch too loudly, for every sound carried clearly in the frosty silence of the Forest. And they had to move very slowly, being careful not to knock any branches and cause the snow to fall with a heavy thump on the ground. It took them over an hour to cover one mile.

At long last, however, they could see, between the trunks of trees, a single light winking like a feeble star. It was coming from inside the King's caravan which stood in a clearing of the Forest. They could see the horse tethered nearby to a tree. The door of the caravan was shut and there was no sign of any smoke from the chimney. But they could hear a murmur of voices and they guessed that Coco and his gang were huddled inside,

shivering, trying to get warmth from one another.

'Are you ready, Great Bear?' whispered Elsewhere softly.

The Great Bear nodded. He removed his scarf and spectacles, handing them to Farmer Thomas. Then he went down on all fours and slowly shuffled forward like an ordinary bear. Snuffling and sniffling, he worked his way round the caravan to the front. Those watching could hear the voices inside suddenly go quiet.

The King's horse whinnied with terror but the Great Bear seemed to say something to it which quietened it.

As he approached the door of the caravan, the Great Bear reared up on his hindlegs and growled deeply in his throat. He began to pound at the wooden panels. He heaved the full weight of his powerful shoulders against the door, splintering it wide open.

Reaching in, he seized one of the clowns by the head and sent him sprawling across the snow. One by one the others jumped out of the caravan, screaming with terror at the sight of what seemed to them a wild bear. They fled into the darkness of the Forest.

There was a pause. No more clowns appeared. And still there was no sign of Coco.

It was now that Elsewhere stepped forward.

At the same moment the bank of clouds overhead slid away and the moon, at three quarters, shone down on the glade, illuminating it like an arena.

As soon as he saw Elsewhere, the Great Bear stepped to one side. Only Elsewhere could confront Coco and rescue the King. That was his task and no one else's.

Elsewhere climbed the steps and stood, framed, in the doorway of the caravan. Inside, at the far end, he could see the King, lying bound and gagged. And there, standing in the centre, waiting for him, was Coco, with a knife in his hand.

Coco smiled. 'The King was right after all,' he observed. 'He said that you would come.'

He paused. Outside they could hear the faint singing of the wind in the trees.

'And now,' said Coco, 'it is between you and me! If you had not appeared on the scene I should have been King, not you. I wonder, can you realise what it means to be deprived, at the last hurdle, of the chance of winning the race? To be way out in front, ahead of everyone, and then suddenly, at the last minute, to be overtaken by a complete outsider!'

His dark eyes glittered in his thin pale face.

Elsewhere stood waiting. He was very moved. After all, Coco was a great artist, and Elsewhere understood very well what he must be feeling. But he knew also that this was no time for sentiment. He knew that Coco was his deadly enemy. If Coco were to kill him, then the King might well have no alternative but to name Coco as his successor. Possibly the King's life, as well as his own, and the future of the clowns, was now in Elsewhere's hands. And his hands were empty. He had no weapon other than his wits.

He stood poised, his eyes on the knife in Coco's hand, his muscles ready for the first movement on the part of his rival. Suddenly Coco charged and, at the same moment, Elsewhere seemed to collapse, to fold under, so that Coco, meeting no obstacle, went flying through the doorway on to the frozen snow outside.

Elsewhere stood up. The first round was his. He was conscious of the King watching alertly in the background, but for the time being all Elsewhere's concentration had to be on Coco.

He climbed down and stood in the moonlit clearing, facing Coco. Just beyond the light, in the shadow of the trees, waited the Great Bear and Odd, Farmer Thomas and his brother Dai, watching the fight between the two clowns.

Slowly each circled the other. The moonlight glinted on the blade of Coco's knife. Each was waiting for the other to make a move. This time it was Elsewhere who

took the initiative. He let out a sharp shrill cry which had a sudden un-nerving effect on Coco. As he hesitated, Elsewhere plunged. He seized hold of Coco's wrist and twisted it sharply so that Coco was thrown off balance. Backwards and forwards they struggled, Elsewhere trying to force him to drop the knife. Now one was on top, now the other. Odd could see the veins bulging on Coco's face and the sweat on Elsewhere's brow. Neither would let go of the other. They seemed almost one body in their movements as each sought for mastery of the knife.

Suddenly, and it was so sudden that those watching gasped, Elsewhere slipped on the frozen snow. The knife plunged and there was a vivid splash of blood on Elsewhere's arm.

Coco stood, breathing heavily, smiling at the blood on the tip of his knife. Again Coco charged and closed with Elsewhere. Again he drew blood. Again and again he charged. Elsewhere crouched, seeming to do nothing. The Great Bear growled dangerously but knew that he must not interfere. Odd looked up anxiously at the moon. He could see the clouds massing again and knew that any moment they might blot out the light from the moon.

The watchers began to shout, urging Elsewhere on. They were disturbed that he seemed to be making no effort. His clothes were slashed, and blood smeared his face. Coco waited, as though taunting him to one last effort before being slaughtered. 'Soon,' he laughed, 'mon pauvre petit, my poor friend, I shall be finished with you as a cat with a mouse. But I shall not kill you. I shall leave you, like Grimaldi, a cripple for the rest of your life!'

Crouching, poised, he moved slowly towards Elsewhere, the knife held in front of him like a spear.

What happened next was so unexpected that it took everyone by surprise. It was almost as though Elsewhere had been waiting, gathering his energy and his concentration for one final blow. With a great bound he leaped sideways into the air and with his feet landed Coco such a blow on the head that the knife was sent spinning out of his hand through the tree tops, while Coco, stunned, was sent sprawling on the ground.

The watchers cheered loudly. The Great Bear, roaring with delight, seized Coco in both arms and holding him high in the air, seemed about to smash his head against a tree trunk when suddenly Elsewhere cried out, 'NO!'

The Great Bear paused, shaking his head as though confused, then hurled Coco slithering across the snow. They watched him crawl forward on his hands and knees. Slowly he dragged himself up and turned to look at Elsewhere, his dark eyes glittering in the moonlight. 'Better a king without friends,' he said bitterly, 'than a King with such an enemy as I!'

He turned and half ran, half limped, until, like his followers, he, too, had disappeared into the Forest and the snow and the darkness.

At that moment the clouds passed over the moon.

Switching on their torches, the watchers moved forward to congratulate Elsewhere, while Farmer Thomas handed the Great Bear his spectacles. As he put them on he chuckled. 'Considering that I'm half blind without them, I didn't do too badly!' He paused and added, 'I must admit I rather enjoyed that!' He turned to Elsewhere. 'Thank you for calling out. I was suddenly consumed with anger and I would have killed him. You are right. It is not necessary.'

Elsewhere climbed into the caravan, followed by Odd, while the others waited outside.

They untied the gag from the King's mouth, and the ropes that bound his ankles and wrists. The King smiled.

'I might have known you two would be inseparable!'

'How are you feeling?' asked Elsewhere, massaging the King's feet.

'I've never felt so useless!' grunted the King in reply. 'However,' he added, cautiously rising to his feet and taking a few steps forward, 'I'm more than ready for your Coronation!'

Elsewhere grinned. He and the King shook hands and embraced. Odd felt a funny gulp in his throat and he turned away. He knew he did not belong here. He jumped down from the caravan and grabbed the Great Bear by the paw. 'Come and meet the King!' he cried.

And Elsewhere, helping the King down the steps by the light of his torch also said, 'Come and meet the Great Bear!'

They spent that night with the Great Bear at Merlin's Chapel. The next morning Farmer Thomas drove them to Tippity House, arranging to return the caravans and the horses later in the day. Elsewhere's wounds had been bathed and bandaged and although he was a little pale, he seemed cheerful and none the worse for his adventures.

Joey was up on the roof of Tippity House, keeping watch, when they arrived, and was the first to see them. He ran to one of the chimneys and shouted down it, '*They're here!*'

The clowns had been seated quietly, having breakfast in the great hall, when they heard his shout echoing down the chimney. At once there was a great hubbub of excitement as they crowded to the front door to greet the King and Elsewhere with loud cheers of welcome.

Throughout the rest of that day Elsewhere rehearsed hard for the Coronation so that it could take place that evening, exactly as had been arranged.

In the Big Top, at Tippity House, the clowns had built a special circular dais in the centre of the ring. The dais was made of platforms, rising one above the other, each one smaller than the one before. On the apex stood the King's throne, a richly carved chair that had once belonged to Grimaldi. Rising out of the dais, and immediately behind the throne, was a Maypole at the top of which many coloured ribbons had been plaited together in an intricate pattern. The pattern had been created especially for the King when he had been crowned, and always for each King a new pattern, and therefore a new dance around the Maypole, was created.

That night, in a hushed silence, the lights were lowered. Every seat was full, the entire Gathering of the Clowns assembled for this, the most important occasion in their lives.

A single light shone down on the old King who sat, crowned, on his throne in the centre of the ring. After a short pause, in a voice full of strength and authority, he proclaimed:

'Let the Un-Crowning commence!'

Immediately, from all sides of the ring which, like the steps of the dais, had been richly carpeted in a deep red, there stepped forward representatives of all the countries throughout the world. These senior clowns had inherited the secret of the Maypole Dance and they, in turn, would hand it on to their successors. As the loose ends of the ribbons were released, fluttering down like streamers, each dancer caught his own and held it taut.

The ribbons radiated out from the pattern at the top of the Maypole like the spokes of a wheel.

The dancers now began to step to a lively tune, weaving in and out. And, as they moved, the ribbons on the Maypole were unplaited. This was known as Reversing the Pattern and was an important part of the Uncrowning of a King. Later, at Elsewhere's crowning, they would dance a new dance and weave a new pattern, which would remain until he ceased to be King and someone else took his place.

When the dance was ended, the tapes were looped up to the canvas walls of the Big top, forming a secondary roof of gaily coloured stripes. The dancers returned to their seats on the edge of the ring.

Now a single note was played on a flute, long and high and questioning, and the King arose to speak once again. Turning to the darkened auditorium, first to one quarter, then to another, and another, he said:

There is one among you who must succeed me!
There is one among you who must wear the crown!
There is one among you who must carry the King's burden!
Let him now declare himself!

As the drums began to roll, a spotlight was turned on to the tiers of crowded seats, moving up and down and across, as though in search of the King's successor. This was to signify that the new King would come from among his own people. At last the spotlight came to rest on Elsewhere who rose, pale but proud. Although all this had been thoroughly rehearsed he found himself shaking with nerves. Softly, yet at the same time in a

voice that could be heard throughout the arena, he said;

I am he who must be King!
I am he must bear the burden!
I am come to uncrown the King!

Slowly he walked down the steps of the auditorium, conscious of all eyes on him, until he was standing at the edge of the carpet which seemed to stretch away and away like a red sea, rising in steps of different shades of red and pink to the throne at the top of the dais.

There stood his old master, waiting for him to come and take the crown from his head and place it on his own, as had been the custom for as long as anyone could remember.

As Elsewhere stepped into the ring, many voices began to sing. It took him by surprise, since when he had rehearsed this part of the ceremony there had been no accompaniment. The music seemed unbearably sad and poignant, yet at the same time noble and proud. It was a Welsh song, sung by the Welsh clowns, about an old bard, a poet, called David of the White Rock, who says farewell to his children for the last time.

As the singing swelled in intensity, Elsewhere began to climb the steps to the throne. He looked up at the large heavy crown resting on the King's head.

Higher and higher he climbed until he felt as though he were climbing a steep cliff face. All round him, out there, in the darkness, rank upon rank, rising up to the roof of the tent, waited his peers, his fellow clowns. They all awaited the solemn moment when he should reach the topmost step of all and seizing the crown from the head of the King firmly place it on his own head.

He had reached the last step, and stood swaying on the edge, not daring to look down. He was surprised to feel sweat sliding down his face. As he reached up his hands to take the crown, the entire Gathering of the Clowns rose to its feet and, with a great roar, cried out the words

King, by your leave!

It was at that moment, just as he was about to take the crown, that Elsewhere collapsed. He fell down the steps, over and over and over, until he lay sprawled on his back at the bottom. There was a gasp of horror throughout the tent. Then the old King slowly came down the steps. At once a great hubbub of conversation broke out, cries of astonishment and dismay that, just at the very moment when Elsewhere was about to become King, this should have happened. Someone was despatched for a stretcher and Elsewhere was carried out of the now silent arena, a still and unconscious figure, covered with a blanket.

Odd grabbed hold of Whizz. 'What happened?' he asked.

'I don't know!' replied Whizz, puzzled.

Throughout that day doctors and specialists kept arriving, and finally Dr Solomon Tump, who had once treated Elsewhere in the past, arrived from London.

Dressed in a black jacket and striped trousers, he opened his brief case and took out a stethoscope. He felt Elsewhere all over, and after much humming and hawing, announced, 'Well, there are no bones broken, but there's no doubt he has a fever, And of course he must have lost quite a bit of blood from these wounds. How did you say he got them? Our first job is to get the patient's temperature down. He'll have to sweat it out. Knowing the patient's past history, I'd say that he has been overdoing things probably. He's the type who lives on his nerves, is easily excited. An enforced rest will do him no harm. Keep him in bed. Change the sheets regularly every time they get soaked with perspiration. Apply ice-packs to his forehead. Try and get him to drink lots of water, he won't be able to eat anything in this condition. While the fever rages he won't be himself or recognise anyone. Then, when he does begin to mend, lots of rest!'

He looked at Odd, smiling quizzically. 'You'll be the best nurse and tonic he can have! By the way, are you still taking your vitamin pills? Let me see, what was it you had before? Ah, yes, here we are' – consulting his notebook, 'Vitmins A,B,C and D. I'll leave a prescription for some fresh supplies for you, and also for Elsewhere when he recovers. We can't have *you* cracking up, you know!' he said kindly, shaking Odd by the paw. And with that he hurried back to London on the next train.

The Coronation had had to be put off and everyone had gone home, except for Whizz, Phizz and Tizz who had stayed behind with Joey to help Odd nurse Elsewhere. They took it in turns, while the fever lasted, to keep watch at his bedside. The Great Bear would drop in to see how Elsewhere was getting along and to have a talk with the King. Often, looking out of the window of Elsewhere's bedroom, Odd would see the Great Bear and the King walking up and down under the trees, deep in conversation.

Mr Goodman and his friend Arbuthnot, who were Odd and Elsewhere's especial friends, drove over from the Granary where they lived. Always, on each visit, they would bring a basket of eggs, or butter, or the honey that had been named, *Odd's Own Honey*.

The King also came daily to sit at Elsewhere's bedside. Day after day Elsewhere lay, recognising no one, his face flushed and feverish, getting thinner and thinner.

'The sickness will leave him very weak,' observed the King.

And then one morning when Odd was sitting by Elsewhere's side, reading a book the Great Bear had lent him, Elsewhere suddenly opened his eyes. He seemed bewildered for a moment, as if he had come from a long way away. Then he saw his friend and smiled.

'*Odd!*' he said.

Odd reached out to embrace him. He could feel the bones through Elsewhere's night-shirt; there was hardly any flesh on him. As though exhausted by the sudden exertion, Elsewhere flopped back on the pillows and lay still. 'Have I been very ill?' he asked.

'Yes,' replied Odd. 'They had to cancel the Coronation and everyone went home except for Whizz, Phizz and Tizz – and Joey – who stayed on to help me nurse you. But there have been letters from all over the world. All the clowns have been asking after you, and there are lots and lots of new stamps for your album! I've saved them all for you.'

Soon, Elsewhere was able to sit up for a few hours each day, wearing a large thick dressing gown that belonged to the King. One day the King called to have a long chat with him.

'I'm sorry I messed up the Coronation,' apologised Elsewhere.

'Don't worry about that,' replied the King. 'The important thing is to get you well and strong.'

'Lying here,' said Elsewhere, 'I've had an awful lot of time to sort things out and to think what kind of person I am and what kind of a King I shall be.

'Things have to change and you have to go with them. I see that now. When you're very young, you're king, you're the most important. You've only got yourself to think about. But then, as you get older, you discover there are a lot of other people who also think they are king!

'I realised that being Elsewhere had been rather fun. Not having to be *here* but *elsewhere,* so that no one could pin me down and say you've got to do this or that. But once I became King I knew I would have to be at people's beck and call all the time. And I thought, once that crown is on my head I'll not be free any more. I'll be trapped. There'll never be any time I can call my own. And I found the thought very frightening, as though I couldn't breathe, and walls were closing in on me!'

'And so you ran away from it by being ill?' observed the King quietly. Elsewhere looked at him.

'Yes, I've run away before, haven't I?' he said. 'I know I run away from things.'

'But you are changing,' said the King. 'You did face responsibility when you had to. You rescued me and you stood up to Coco who was your enemy. Perhaps I should say *is* your enemy. For he will turn up again, and that

will be a problem you will have to deal with on your own when the time comes.'

The King got up to put some more coal on the fire. 'Do you remember,' he said, 'a long time ago I told you that when the time came for you to succeed me I would teach you the Secret of Tippity-Witchit? That secret which is handed down from one King to another?'

Elsewhere nodded; his eyes grave and thoughtful.

'That secret,' said the King, 'which every clown has to learn but which the King must always know, is how to perform even when he doesn't feel like performing. The clown learns, as in Grimaldi's famous song of Tippity-Witchit, which I shall teach you, how to make faces so as to make people laugh. Even if his own heart is breaking, the clown must go on and perform. Because the clown's task is to make people laugh. Laughter is a great medicine and people always need laughter.

'You know how much Grimaldi used to suffer from moods and depressions – you learn that as a young clown in your history lessons – so you will remember the day he went to see a doctor about his depressions. The Doctor didn't know who he was and he said to Grimaldi, "The best tonic I can recommend for you is a good laugh. Go and see Grimaldi perform!"

'Grimaldi himself used to joke about this and say to his friends, "I am *Grim-all-day* but at night I am *Grimaldi* and I make you laugh!" The King of the Clowns has to set an example to all the others and must never reveal his own worries or problems. Those he must keep to himself.'

At that moment there was a knock on the door and Joey popped his head round to say, 'They're all ready!'

'Just ask them to wait a few moments, will you, Joey?'

replied the King. Elsewhere could hear whisperings outside on the landing and then the door closed again.

'What is it?' he asked.

'Now that you're almost well,' answered the King, 'I thought we would finish the Coronation. You've done everything except the final act of taking the crown off my head and putting it on yours. And I thought we would do it here, in front of the fire, quite informally, with a few friends. Afterwards we'll have supper to celebrate your finally becoming King!'

Into the room came Whizz, Phizz and Tizz, little Joey, Wiggee and Bloggs, Mr Goodman and Arbuthnot, the Great Bear with Taliesin perched on his shoulder, Farmer Thomas and Mrs Thomas and their seven children, and his brother Dai. Some perched on the bed, some sat on the floor, in fact wherever they could find a space to sit.

'It's quite a family gathering,' laughed Elsewhere.

'Yes,' replied the King. 'I thought you might prefer that. We also tried to get Hallelujah and Collander Moll but they wrote, sending their love, saying they couldn't come because there were "things going on at Fenton House".'

'Things going on at Fenton House?' repeated Odd. 'I wonder what that can mean!'

There was a sudden hush as the King lifted the crown and placed it on his head. As Elsewhere stood up and reached out to lift the crown, the clowns in the room, but not the visitors, shouted out;

King, by your leave!

Elsewhere placed the crown on his own head. It was much heavier than he had realised and it was also a bit big for him.

'We'll have to get it altered to fit you properly,' said the old King. 'Right! Now let's have supper. Everything ready, Bloggs?'

Bloggs nodded and led the way downstairs where a table had been drawn up in front of the great fireplace. They sat down to a simple supper of Welsh rarebit, sausage and mash, cups of tea, and Christmas pudding.

'I have a feeling,' remarked the old King to Elsewhere, 'that, as King, you may decide to do things in a different way. Much more simply. So I told Bloggs to make it a family supper. I hope that's all right, *your Majesty!*'

Elsewhere, who was nibbling the end of a sausage skewered on his fork, grinned.

'I like the other way, too,' he said. 'But it's fun doing things differently from time to time so that people never know quite what to expect!'

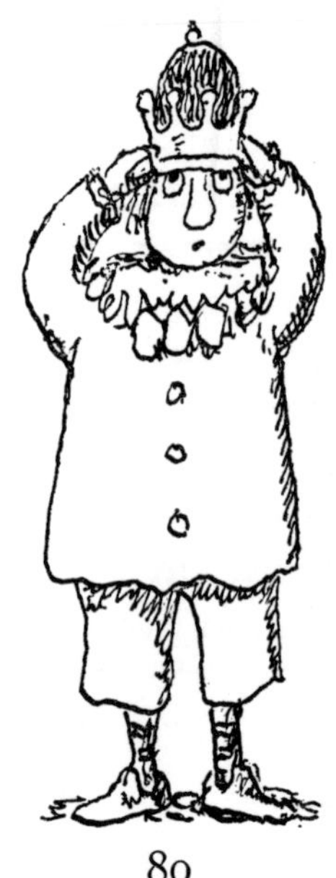

A few days later Odd and Elsewhere prepared to set off on their return journey to London. Elsewhere had to see Dr Solomon Tump for a final check up after which, if all was well, he was to set off on his travels around the world, visiting Germany first. Whizz, Phizz and Tizz had already gone ahead to make preparations. They were very proud that the German clowns were to be the first to receive a visit from Elsewhere as King.

The old King bowed low before Elsewhere as he said goodbye.

'I'm going to stay at the Granary with Mr Goodman and Arbuthnot,' he said. 'And the Great Bear has also invited me to stay with him whenever I want. I daresay I shall roam around until I find a place to settle.'

'Won't you miss all this?' asked Elsewhere, pointing to Tippity House.

'Not really,' replied the old King. 'You see, as King, you will find you are hardly ever here but always elsewhere, if you will pardon the pun! For the greater part of the year you will be travelling about, visiting other clowns, as well as performing. This place is not really home in the way that the Granary is for Mr Goodman or Fenton House has been for you. You'll find the King's caravan, which is yours now, much more comfortable when you have to stay here. This is a house for special occasions like the Gatherings. It's more like a museum for clowns.'

Odd looked across at Elsewhere as the old King said this and they both grinned. They had not forgotten Elsewhere's resolve to find the missing collection of Grimaldi's butterflies and to present it to Tippity House to be exhibited alongside all the other relics of Grimaldi. The old King noticed the look that the two friends exchanged and said, 'What's this, secrets? Always have something up your sleeve, a few surprises! I shall look forward to being a visitor from time to time and seeing what changes you will have made!'

Arbuthnot opened the door of his ancient car for the King to get in. Then, with a great revving of the engine, and a snorting and belching of smoke, the car drove off.

The snows had all gone and there was a smell of spring in the air. Tipsy whinnied as though she were impatient to be leaving. The two friends said goodbye to Joey, who was being left in charge of Tippity House while Elsewhere was on his travels. Lastly they shook hands with the Great Bear who had come along to see them off.

In the early morning silence they could hear robins and chaffinches singing. The Great Bear, turning to Odd, said, 'Elsewhere has now entered into his kingdom. You have yet to enter into yours. But the time is approaching when you and I shall have much to do, little one. Until we meet again, I wish you both safe journeying!'

Thus Odd and Elsewhere set off on their long journey back to London.

When they arrived at Fenton House they were surprised to find it covered on the outside with scaffolding and polythene sheeting.

'So that's what Collander Moll meant by "things going on",' observed Elsewhere.

'Oh, look!' cried Odd. 'Do you see? They are doing something to the roof.'

All the tiles had been removed and were stacked in small piles like sandwiches, balanced on the lathes which stretched horizontally along the roof.

In front of the house was a high wire fence and an official looking notice which announced:

Round the back the first person they bumped into was Collander Moll. She had several more wigs pinned on her head, and she seemed even larger than usual.

'What's happening?' they cried, as they saw workmen moving in and out.

'Dad and me's having to camp out,' she replied. 'So I'm wearing all my clothes. I feel like a travelling wardrobe. I dunno where your things are – there's topsy-turvy the whole place is!'

'But *what is happening?*' they asked again.

Everywhere there were bags of cement. Carpets had been taken up, leaving brown and decaying old newspapers underneath. Water went *spit-pit-pat* from holes in ceilings into buckets placed underneath. Curtains had been looped up and the ends knotted.

'Has there been a bomb?' asked Odd. 'Has someone tried to blow us up?'

'Not a bomb, silly!' laughed Collander Moll. 'It's just that they have discovered the old house is in urgent need of repairs. It's going to have a face-lift. Well, mark my words, it's me who could do with a face-lift! They're putting on a new roof, new chimneys, new windows. And they say that all the old plumbing is obsolete.'

'What's obsolete?' asked Odd.

'It's what I am!' replied Collander Moll. 'Worn out and obsolete! Oh, and something else! They're going to put in new central heating and also what they call a *hu-mid-i-fic-ation* system.' She said the word slowly, syllable by syllable.

'What does that mean?' asked Elsewhere.

'It means a cooling system. So that when we've been warmed up, we can be cooled off! Why they can't leave things alone, I don't know! A waste of money, if you ask me. And the National Trust has launched a public appeal for the money.' As she talked, she was busy moving things from one place to another, getting in more of a muddle all the time.

'You should read what the surveyor had to say!' she snorted. 'It's like a doctor's report. You wonder how we managed to live here all these years. They say there's "rising damp and suspicious looking cracks in the ceiling"; oh, and that the main staircase must be "put in order". As though it had been misbehaving!'

The back door slammed, and Hallelujah Jones entered with an armful of potted plants.

'*And* they say the south corner of the garden is to be re-organised and landscaped!' he growled, overhearing Moll. 'Do they think the south corner had been *dis*-organised then! And what do they mean, *landscaped*? I know them fancy landscape gardeners: they work it all out on paper. Paper gardening, that's what it is! Never been near a plant in their lives, most of them.

'A garden doesn't have to be organised,' he continued. 'It has a way of its own and you have to get to know it. Every garden's different and you can't force it to go the way it doesn't want to go. Same as people. They think they can straighten people out, just like that. But they can't!'

'It's like they say all the floor beams and joists in the house are crooked,' added Collander Moll. 'I suppose they're going to straighten them out as well!'

'And then they'll be surprised when the whole house falls down!' chuckled Hallelujah. 'Serve them right if it did!'

With that he stomped off, carrying the potted plants to the greenhouse at the end of the garden.

'There's real upset is Dad!' sighed Moll. 'You can see the state he's in. Not that I'm much better!' she added, pinning on her several wigs more securely. 'And I dunno where you two are going to sleep. There's workmen up in the attics, re-wiring; and the roof is half off, great gales blowing up there. You'd both be a lot safer down here.'

'We shall sleep in our caravan, of course!' replied Odd.

'I don't know why you don't move into a hotel!' retorted Collander Moll, slamming the door behind her.

The two friends looked at each other in amazement.

'Did you notice,' said Odd, 'neither of them asked about the Coronation? Or whether you were really better now?'

'Grown-ups are like that sometimes,' remarked Elsewhere quietly. 'I shouldn't let it worry you.'

Odd looked at him, suddenly sensing in Elsewhere a new authority. Since his illness he had become a much calmer person, more thoughtful and less of a show-off.

'Yes, you're right,' replied Odd. 'They've got their own worries. If only we could help in some way!'

'Shall we go upstairs and have a look at our room?' suggested Elsewhere.

'Oh, yes, let's!' cried Odd, clapping his paws excitedly.

Odd and Elsewhere climbed up the main staircase, peering in all the rooms on their way. There were tea-chests marked 'China from the two fitted alcoves in drawing room', or, 'Chandelier from the Blue Room'. Shutters had been drawn across windows so that only strips of daylight filtered through. Furniture and musical instruments, crowded into two rooms and shrouded with dust-sheets, looked like icebergs. Marble busts of old fashioned men and women, no longer on their pedestals, had been shoved under a grand piano, alongside fenders and old notices saying 'Please do not touch'. Stacked against the walls, like large playing cards, were paintings in gilt frames, leaving on the walls clean patches where they had hung.

Their own attic room was empty, and wire dangled from holes in the walls. They could hear the workmen on the roof. Odd opened the door of the cupboard where they usually kept all their things, such as Elsewhere's stamp album and his collection of honey jars and gasped.

'What is it?' asked Elsewhere, joining him.

'Look!' cried Odd.

The back of the cupboard had been knocked through and there, revealed behind the broken panelling, was a steep staircase.

'You go first,' suggested Odd. He thought there might be bats up there and he was nervous. So Elsewhere led the way. The steps were very shallow and black with soot-like dirt. The next moment their faces were on a level with the floor above. They found themselves in a tent-like space which was the steeply sloping roof of Fenton House. There were chinks of daylight, and wind blowing through the eaves.

'We're in the eaves,' said Elsewhere. 'Listen! Can you hear? It's raining.'

The loft seemed to be sub-divided by partitions into smaller tents in which they found tiny fire-places, or an iron bed, or hooks in a beam for hanging clothes.

'People must have slept here once,' observed Elsewhere.

'Just imagine sleeping up here!' added Odd. 'It must have been very draughty.'

They discovered that the loft was like a corridor on four sides. In the centre was a square built brick structure.

'Do you think it is the chimney stack?' asked Odd.

'Or perhaps it's a secret room!' suggested Elsewhere. He paused. 'Hullo! Have you seen this?'

At the head of the small staircase that led up from their room was a tiny door set into the brick structure. Elsewhere tried to turn the handle but it would not move. Then Odd had a go. He tugged and tugged but still it would not open.

'I tell you what,' said Elsewhere. 'I don't think it's the kind of handle that turns. I think it's just that the door is stuck. It probably hasn't been opened for many years. If you put your arms round my waist as I pull, and if we both pull really hard, then perhaps it will open? Are you ready?'

Odd stood behind Elsewhere, clasping his paws tightly together.

'Ready!' he said.

'Right!' replied Elsewhere. 'Ready, steady – *pull*!'

And together they pulled. There was a loud crack as though something had split. The door jerked open so suddenly that they fell backwards, and the two friends found themselves staring into a small, dark room.

'Do you think it really is a secret room?' whispered Odd.

'Perhaps there's hidden treasure!' suggested Elsewhere.

'And it might be worth millions of pounds!' said Odd.

'And billions!' laughed Elsewhere.

'And trillions!' capped Odd.

They climbed through the small doorway.

'That's strange!' said Elsewhere. 'Everywhere else the roof slopes, but here, in this room, it's flat. Do you see?' He pointed to the ceiling above them. 'Can you hear the rain drumming down on it? That's how you can tell it's flat on the outside as well. Perhaps it was once a courtyard here, among the rooftops, right in the centre, and then perhaps later it was filled in to make an extra room to store things in.'

'Ouch!' cried Odd suddenly.

'What is it?' asked Elsewhere.

'I don't know!' giggled Odd who had knocked his funny bone. 'Perhaps it's your treasure!'

'Let's have a look!' cried Elsewhere.

Odd had bumped into a tall wooden chest with many small drawers. It was very heavy and they had to heave and shove it until they had got it into the light and could see it properly.

'I wonder what's in it?' said Odd. 'The drawers are not like ordinary drawers. They're much narrower.'

Gently Elsewhere pulled one open. Then another. And another. The wood had swollen with the damp and the drawers were stiff. He opened all the drawers one after the other.

Each one contained a large frame of pinned butterflies.

The two friends looked at each other in amazement.

'I wonder where they have come from?' murmured Elsewhere, looking at the back of one of the frames. And then he cried softly, 'Oh, Odd, look!'

Odd peered at the thin, faded writing, in brown ink, and read:

Clouded Yellows
Found Sussex Downs
June 13th. 1819

and underneath was the signature

Jos Grimaldi

The two friends stood in silence, gazing at each other. They could hear the shouts of the workmen knocking off for lunch, and the rain drumming down steadily.

'It's Grimaldi's lost collection of butterflies!' murmured Elsewhere in awe.

'And you've found it!' said Odd. 'Just like you said you would! But fancy it's being here all the time!'

They looked at the back of each of the frames and found, in the same handwriting, Grimaldi's notes on the different butterflies: their identification, and the date and place where caught. Sometimes he had initialled the notes, J.G. and on others he had written his full name, Joseph Grimaldi, or else Jos. Grimaldi.

'But how on earth can they have got here?' said Elsewhere.

'Do you think the thieves hid them here?' suggested Odd.

'Or perhaps,' said Elsewhere, 'the person who hid them here died without telling anyone where they were hidden. I might have searched and searched and never thought of finding them right above our own room! They might never have been found at all if Fenton House had not had to be repaired.'

'And if we had not been curious to know where that door led!' added Odd.

'One should always open closed doors!' replied Elsewhere with a grin.

A Tippity-Witchit or Pantomimical Paroxysms

first sung by Joseph Grimaldi in July, 1811 at Sadlers Wells Theatre in *Bang Up or Harlequin Prince.*

This very morning handy
My malady was such,
And in my tea took brandy
And took a drop too much

HICCUPS Chorus: Tol de rol Fol de rol, And Diddy-i-aye!

Now I'm quite drowsy growing,
For this very morn,
I rose while cock was crowing –
Excuse me if I yawn!

YAWNS, HICCUPS Chorus: Tol de rol etc.

But stop, I mustn't wag hard,
My head aches! If you please,
One pinch of Irish blackguard*
I'll take to give me ease.

*Snuff

SNEEZES, YAWNS, HICCUPS Chorus: Tol de rol etc.

I'm not in cue for frolic,
Can't up my spirits keep.
Love's a windy colic
Tis that makes me weep.

CRIES, SNEEZES, YAWNS, HICCUPS Chorus: Tol de rol etc.

I'm not in mood for crying!
Care's a silly calf.
If to get fat you're trying,
The only way's to laugh!

LAUGHS, CRIES, SNEEZES, YAWNS, HICCUPS Chorus: Tol de rol etc.

Grimaldi, with feet turned in, arms akimbo, used to sneeze, yawn, cry, and roar with laughter, twisting his face into every *type* of *twitch* imaginable, after which he would give his celebrated screeching peals of laughter that would echo and re-echo throughout the theatre.